WHEN
TREE
BECAME A
TREE

ROB HODGSON

RISE

NEW YORK

For Grandma

—RH

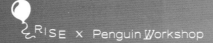 RISE × Penguin Workshop

An imprint of Penguin Random House LLC
1745 Broadway, New York, New York 10019

First published in the United States of America by Rise × Penguin Workshop,
an imprint of Penguin Random House LLC, 2025

Visit us online at penguinrandomhouse.com.

Library of Congress Cataloging-in-Publication Data is available.

Manufactured in China

ISBN 9780593886694   10 9 8 7 6 5 4 3 2 1 HH

The text is set in AauxPro OT.
This art was created with traditional media and an iPad, and assembled in Photoshop.

Edited by Nicole Fox
Designed by Maria Elias

CONTENTS

CHAPTER 1
SEED

This is a forest.

It is home to many different types of trees.

One of those trees is an apple tree.

One day, an apple falls from the tree and rolls onto the forest floor.

Wheeee!

Over time, the apple softens and breaks
down, until all that's left is a single seed.

Seed snuggles into the cozy ground and
sleeps through the cold winter.

Look! Here come our friends
Sun and Cloud.

Sun brings light and warmth to the forest,
and Cloud brings rainwater.

With their help, Seed has everything she needs
to wake up and start growing!

CHAPTER 2

SPROUT

Seed is hungry after her long sleep, so she grows a root that goes down into the ground to find water and food.

She finds some! Her root sucks them up like a straw.

As Seed eats, she begins to get fuller . . .

and fuller . . .

until she pops off her seed covering, and sprouts!

She stretches her new sprout up toward Sun's light and unfolds her first leaves, becoming a Seedling.

CHAPTER 3

PHOTOSYNTHESIS

Seedling keeps eating and growing more leaves. When her leaves are large enough, they help Seedling do something amazing: MAKE HER OWN FOOD!

Psst . . . When I make food, it's called *photosynthesis.*

Seedling makes food by
first soaking in sunlight
through her leaves.

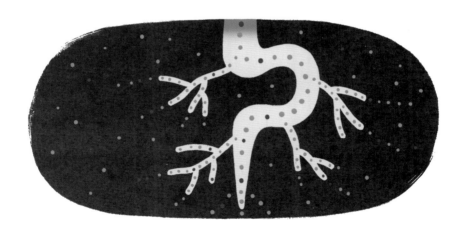

Then she slurps up some
water from the ground.

Finally, her leaves breathe in
an invisible gas from the air,
called carbon dioxide.

Mmm . . .
Tastes like sunshine!

While Seedling makes food,
her leaves breathe out a different invisible gas
into the air, called oxygen.

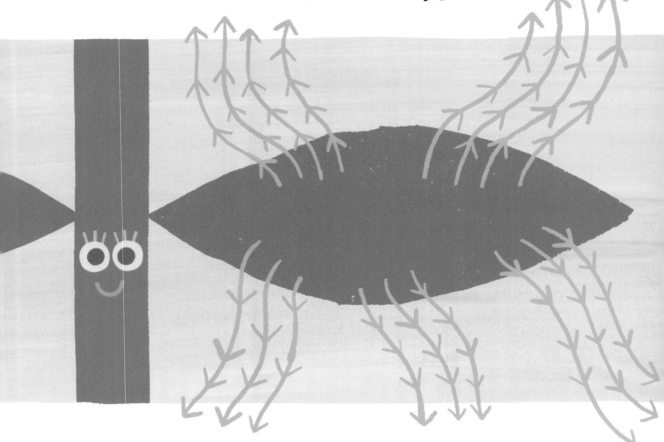

Oxygen isn't just any gas, though. It's what
humans and animals breathe in to live!

Seedling is very helpful.

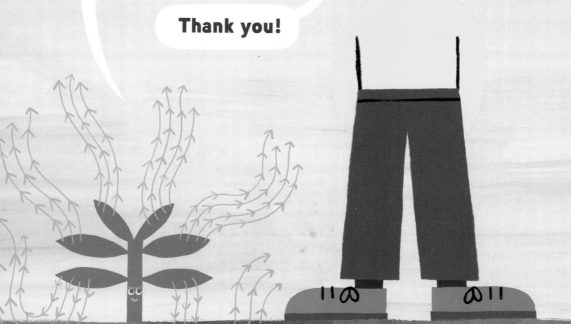

Here's a breath of fresh air!

Thank you!

CHAPTER 4

TREE

Seedling makes a lot of food with her new leaves.

She's made so much that she has grown!

Now she has lots of branches reaching out in different directions to get as much of Sun's light as possible.

As she grows outward, Seedling's stem hardens
into a tough trunk that keeps her safe and strong.

After much growing, she's no longer just
a seedling—she's a young tree!

CHAPTER 5
PUTTING DOWN ROOTS

Tree loves being a tree.

Over the years, she extends
her roots deeper and wider,
searching for more tasty
things in the ground.

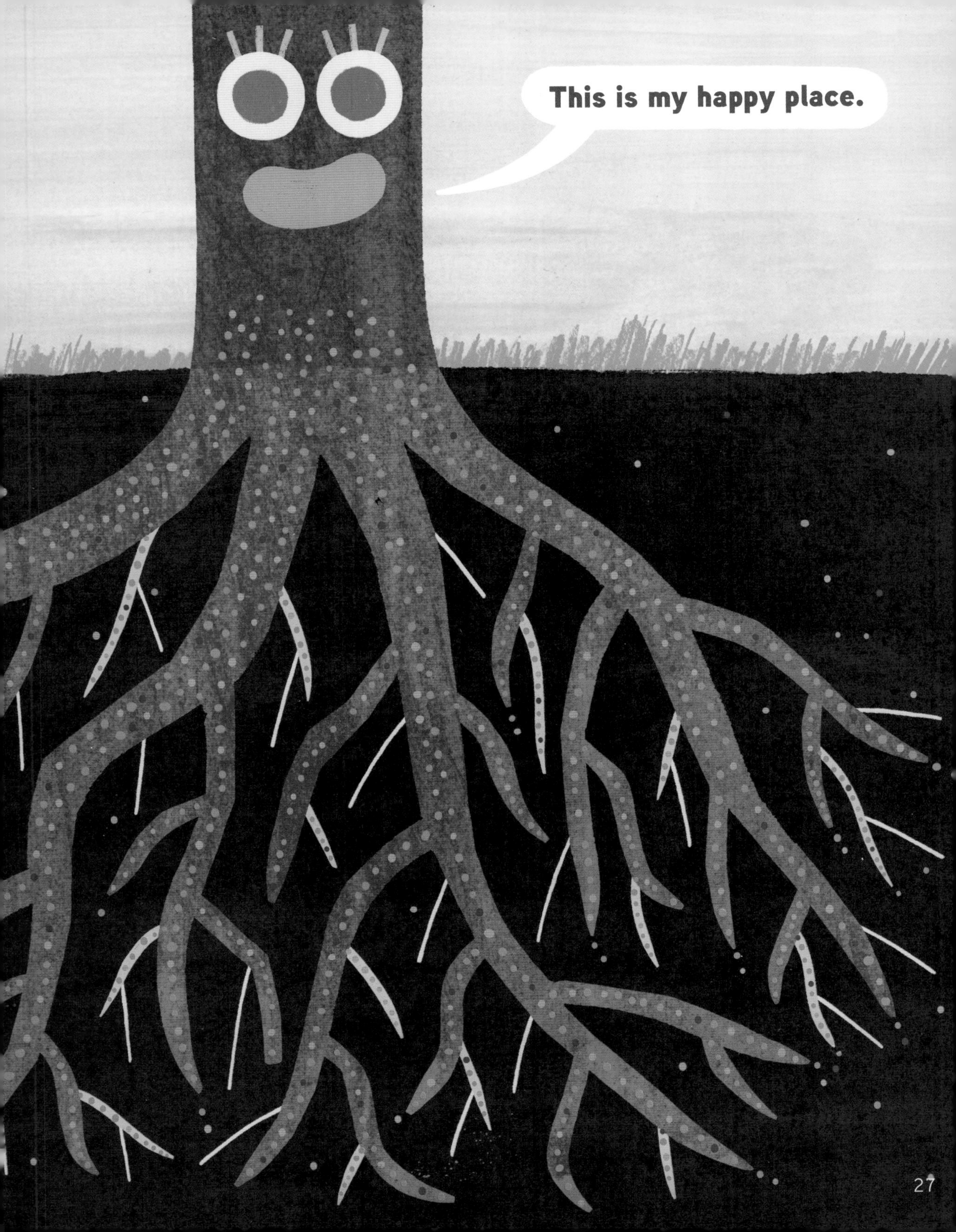
This is my happy place.

Here comes Wind!

He blows as strong as he can,
but Tree is prepared: Her roots
hold her firmly in the ground.

29

Tree's roots do more than just hold her in place and find food and water.

They spread deep beneath the ground to meet with the roots of other trees!

This lets Tree "talk" to her close neighbors. Trees have a lot to talk about.

Tree wonders if she can talk to other trees farther away. She can!

Beneath the ground, mushrooms and other fungi make special threads, called mycelia, that connect all the plants and trees together.

Tree loves connecting to these threads through her roots so that she can hear the forest news.

Rain is coming!

Watch out for bugs!

CHAPTER 6

FAMILY

Tree has many forest friends, but she also has
a big tree family around the world.

In faraway rainforests, durian trees grow
special, smelly fruits.

On mountain slopes, there are pine trees
with spiky needles for leaves.

There are weeping willow trees in
city parks, with long branches that
sway gently in the breeze.

And all kinds of trees with shapes
of their own, like this baobab tree
that lives in dry plains. Tree loves
her big, special family.

CHAPTER 7
SPRING

Tree doesn't always look the same. In fact,
she likes to change every season! The way
she looks depends on how much of Sun's
light she gets in each season.

In the spring, when Sun is shining bright,
something magical happens to Tree's
branches: They grow tiny buds!

After a few weeks, they begin to
open up slowly, until, one by one,
they reveal . . .

40

Bees love Tree's flowers. They like to drink a special juice from the flowers called nectar and collect a fuzzy dust called pollen.

When they travel to different flowers and plants, they carry and spread Tree's pollen. They also share nectar with other bees. It's a pollen party!

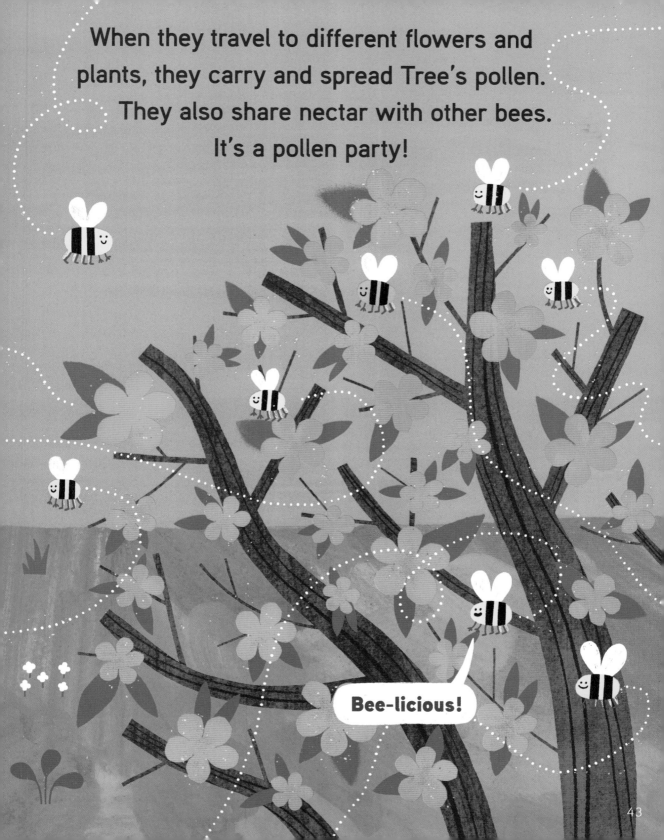

CHAPTER 8

SUMMER

When other pollen mixes with Tree's flowers,
fruit begins to grow.

Throughout the sunny days of summer,
Tree grows lots of apples!

Other trees have grown their own fruits,
and some have even grown nuts.

The forest is full of surprises!

Tree is proud of her apples
and loves to share.

47

CHAPTER 9

AUTUMN

When autumn arrives, Sun starts to
tuck away earlier in the day, letting
Tree know it's time to rest.

Since there's less of Sun's light, Tree will
let go of her leaves to save energy.

Before she snuggles in for a winter's rest,
Tree puts on one final show . . .

. . . turning her leaves bright
orange, red, and gold.

51

CHAPTER 10

WINTER

One by one, Tree's leaves float away,
leaving her branches bare.

During the winter, Tree doesn't grow new leaves, but she does put down some more roots to find a little extra food, keep steady, and talk with her friends.

I'm getting comfy!

Tree loves each season, and she grows bigger

and wiser with each passing year.

CHAPTER 11

THE GRAND TREE

Tree has now lived through
many changing seasons.

In fact, she's lived eighty years!

Some of her branches fall to the ground,
making cozy homes for critters.

Over time, they break down, making the
ground a better place for new trees to grow.

Tree knows her transformation will bring
new life to the forest.

59

CHAPTER 12

NEW LIFE

Look! One of Tree's last apples falls
and rolls away.

Over time, the apple breaks down,
leaving behind a sleepy little seed.

With some help from our friends
Sun and Cloud,

Seed grows roots, and leaves,
and eventually turns into . . .